Tagliatelle Pasta Cookbook

Delicious Tagliatelle Pasta Recipes for Every Occasion

TAGLIATELLE PASTA COOKBOOK

First edition. November 11, 2023.

ISBN: 979-8215036266

Written by john ahmad.

John Ahmad

Chapter Outline:

Introduction to Tagliatelle Pasta

- History and origin of tagliatelle pasta
- Varieties of tagliatelle pasta

Essential Tools and Ingredients

- Must-have kitchen tools for making tagliatelle
- Types of flour and eggs for the perfect tagliatelle dough

Mastering Tagliatelle Dough

- Step-by-step guide to making homemade tagliatelle dough
- Tips for achieving the ideal dough consistency

Classic Tagliatelle Recipes

- Traditional tagliatelle alfredo
- Creamy carbonara with tagliatelle
- Bolognese tagliatelle

Fresh and Light Tagliatelle Dishes

- Lemon and herb tagliatelle
- Spinach and ricotta stuffed tagliatelle
- Mediterranean-inspired tagliatelle salad

Gourmet Tagliatelle Creations

- Truffle-infused tagliatelle
- Lobster and champagne tagliatelle
- Wild mushroom and thyme tagliatelle

Sauces that Elevate Tagliatelle

- Homemade marinara sauce
- Pesto perfection with tagliatelle
- Creamy gorgonzola and walnut sauce

Seafood Lovers' Tagliatelle

- Shrimp scampi tagliatelle
- Scallop and saffron tagliatelle
- Smoked salmon and dill tagliatelle

Comforting Tagliatelle Casseroles

- Chicken and broccoli tagliatelle bake
- Beef and mushroom tagliatelle casserole
- Creamy spinach and artichoke tagliatelle

International Twists on Tagliatelle

- Thai-inspired peanut tagliatelle
- Indian masala tagliatelle
- Chinese-style sesame ginger tagliatelle

Vegan and Vegetarian Tagliatelle Delights

- Vegan cashew cream tagliatelle
- Roasted vegetable tagliatelle
- Eggplant and sun-dried tomato tagliatelle

Quick and Easy Tagliatelle Meals

- One-pan garlic butter tagliatelle
- Tagliatelle primavera
- Speedy weeknight sausage and pepper tagliatelle

Fresh Homemade Sauces

- Roasted red pepper and tomato sauce
- Creamy basil and pine nut sauce
- Caramelized onion and balsamic reduction

Tagliatelle for Special Occasions

- Holiday truffle and herb tagliatelle
- Anniversary lobster tagliatelle
- Elegant champagne cream tagliatelle

Artisanal Flavored Tagliatelle Variations

- Beetroot-infused tagliatelle
- Squid ink tagliatelle
- Saffron and sun-dried tomato tagliatelle

Tagliatelle from Scratch: Advanced Techniques

- Colored and flavored pasta doughs
- Rolled and filled tagliatelle variations

Gluten-Free Tagliatelle Options

- Making gluten-free tagliatelle dough
- Gluten-free sauce options

Leftover Remix: Creative Tagliatelle Recipes

- Tagliatelle frittata
- Tagliatelle-stuffed bell peppers
- Tagliatelle panzanella salad

Sweet Endings with Tagliatelle

- Dessert tagliatelle with berries and mascarpone
- Chocolate hazelnut tagliatelle nests
- Cinnamon sugar tagliatelle crisps

Chapter 1: Introduction to Tagliatelle Pasta

Tagliatelle pasta, with its long, elegant ribbons, holds a special place in Italian culinary heritage. In this chapter, we delve into the rich history and diverse varieties of tagliatelle pasta, exploring the origins that have made it a beloved staple on tables around the world.

History and Origin of Tagliatelle Pasta

The story of tagliatelle's creation is steeped in legend and romance, adding a touch of intrigue to its culinary allure. While historical records can be elusive, one of the most charming tales attributes tagliatelle's invention to a moment of inspiration during a Renaissance wedding feast.

Legend has it that tagliatelle was created in 1487 in honor of the wedding between Lucrezia Borgia and Alfonso d'Este. A skilled chef from Bologna, inspired by the beauty of Lucrezia's blonde hair, is said to have fashioned the flat ribbons of tagliatelle to resemble her locks. Whether a myth or a historical fact, this origin story adds a touch of romance to the pasta's beginnings.

As the centuries passed, tagliatelle gained culinary significance, becoming a cherished dish in the Emilia-Romagna region of Italy. Early cookbooks provide evidence of tagliatelle's presence, showcasing its enduring popularity and ability to adapt to changing culinary trends.

Culinary Traditions

Tagliatelle's presence in culinary records dates back centuries, showcasing its enduring popularity. Early cookbooks from the region of Emilia-Romagna, particularly Bologna, provide evidence of tagliatelle as a cherished dish. Its simple yet flavorful nature, along with its ability to hold a variety of sauces, contributed to its place in Italian cuisine.

The process of making tagliatelle became a tradition in itself, passed down through generations of Italian families. Grandmothers and mothers would share their expertise with younger generations, ensuring that the art of crafting tagliatelle lived on.

Cultural Significance

Beyond its culinary attributes, tagliatelle holds cultural significance. In Bologna, the home of tagliatelle, there's a sense of pride associated with the pasta. It symbolizes the city's dedication to gastronomy and craftsmanship. Over time, tagliatelle has become not just a dish but an emblem of Italian culinary heritage.

Tagliatelle has also found its way into literature, art, and popular culture, further solidifying its place in the hearts of Italians and food enthusiasts around the world. Festivals and events celebrating tagliatelle are a testament to its enduring popularity and its ability to bring people together.

Varieties of Tagliatelle Pasta

While the classic tagliatelle is a marvel in itself, culinary creativity has given rise to several exciting variations, each with its own unique characteristics.

Traditional Tagliatelle

The quintessential tagliatelle is a marvel of simplicity and elegance. Made with just eggs and flour, rolled thin, and cut into fine ribbons, it has a delicate texture that pairs harmoniously with a variety of sauces. Its slightly porous surface allows sauces to cling lovingly to each strand, creating a harmonious marriage of flavors.

Colored Creations

Infusing tagliatelle dough with natural ingredients creates a stunning spectrum of colors and flavors. Spinach adds a vibrant green, while beets impart a deep red hue. Squid ink introduces a striking black variation that not only looks captivating but also brings a hint of brininess to the pasta. These colored tagliatelle variations not only add visual appeal to dishes but also showcase the endless possibilities that pasta-making offers.

Stuffed Delights

Tagliatelle's versatility extends to the realm of stuffed pasta. Skilled hands can lovingly encase fillings within the pasta, creating pockets of delectable surprises. From ricotta and spinach to rich meat fillings, these variations add a layer of complexity to the tagliatelle experience. The interplay between the tender pasta and the savory fillings is a testament to the creativity and craftsmanship of Italian cuisine.

Gluten-Free Options

For those with dietary restrictions, there's no need to miss out on the tagliatelle experience. By carefully selecting gluten-free flours and mastering the art of dough handling, it's possible to create tagliatelle that's every bit as satisfying and flavorful as the traditional version. The gluten-free tagliatelle retains its signature texture and serves as a canvas for an array of delightful sauces, ensuring that everyone can enjoy this beloved pasta.

From its captivating origin story to its various interpretations, tagliatelle pasta has truly made its mark in the culinary landscape. As we embark on this culinary journey, remember that each forkful of tagliatelle brings with it a taste of history and a world of possibilities. Whether you're savoring the classic preparation or embracing innovative variations, tagliatelle is a testament to the art of pasta-making and a celebration of Italy's rich culinary heritage.

Chapter 2: Essential Tools and Ingredients

In the world of tagliatelle pasta, crafting the perfect dish requires a harmony of ingredients and the right tools. In this chapter, we'll explore the essential kitchen tools you need to master the art of tagliatelle-making, as well as the key types of flour and eggs that form the foundation of the perfect tagliatelle dough.

Must-Have Kitchen Tools for Making Tagliatelle

Before you embark on your tagliatelle-making journey, it's important to equip your kitchen with the necessary tools that will elevate your pasta-making experience to new heights.

Rolling Pin: An indispensable tool for flattening and thinning the pasta dough to achieve the desired thickness for tagliatelle.

Pasta Machine: While not mandatory, a pasta machine simplifies the process of rolling and cutting the dough into consistent tagliatelle ribbons.

Bench Scraper or Knife: Essential for cutting the rolled-out dough into elegant tagliatelle strips.

Mixing Bowls: Used for combining and kneading the dough ingredients.

Measuring Cups and Spoons: Precise measurements ensure consistent results.

Large Cutting Board or Clean Work Surface: Provides ample space for rolling and cutting the dough.

Drying Rack: If making homemade tagliatelle, a drying rack prevents the strands from sticking together as they air dry.

Pasta Pot: For cooking the tagliatelle to perfection.

Colander: Used to drain the cooked pasta.

Saucepan: For preparing delicious tagliatelle sauces.

Tongs or Pasta Fork: Handy for gently tossing and serving cooked tagliatelle.

Fine-Mesh Strainer: Useful for dusting flour and ensuring an even coating on the dough.

Types of Flour and Eggs for the Perfect Tagliatelle Dough

The foundation of exceptional tagliatelle lies in the dough, and selecting the right flour and eggs is paramount.

Flour: The type of flour you use determines the texture and flavor of your tagliatelle. "Tipo 00" flour is commonly used in Italy for making pasta due to its fine texture and high protein content. Semolina flour, with its coarser texture, can add a rustic touch to your tagliatelle.

Eggs: Fresh, high-quality eggs are essential. They not only provide structure and flavor but also contribute to the golden color of the dough. Eggs from pasture-raised chickens can lend an exceptional richness to your tagliatelle.

Egg-to-Flour Ratio: Achieving the perfect balance of eggs to flour is crucial. A typical ratio is around 1 egg for every 100 grams of flour, but slight adjustments may be necessary based on factors like humidity and flour type.

Mastering the Tagliatelle Dough

Creating the ideal tagliatelle dough is an art that requires attention to detail and a tactile understanding of the ingredients. From mixing to kneading, resting to rolling, each step contributes to the final texture and taste of the pasta.

Mixing the Ingredients: Learn the proper technique for combining flour and eggs to form a shaggy dough.

Kneading: Discover the rhythmic process of kneading, which develops gluten and imparts elasticity to the dough.

Resting: Understand the importance of allowing the dough to rest, enabling the gluten to relax and making it easier to roll out.

Rolling and Cutting: Whether using a rolling pin or a pasta machine, master the art of achieving the perfect thickness and cutting the dough into uniform tagliatelle strips.

By equipping yourself with the right tools and selecting quality ingredients, you're setting the stage for a tagliatelle-making adventure that's bound to yield delicious results. As we move forward, remember that the heart of a memorable tagliatelle dish begins with the careful selection of tools, flour, and eggs, and the meticulous crafting of the perfect dough.

Chapter 3: Mastering Tagliatelle Dough

In the art of tagliatelle-making, the dough serves as the canvas upon which flavors are layered and experiences are crafted. In this chapter, we embark on a step-by-step journey, guiding you through the process of creating homemade tagliatelle dough. We'll also explore essential tips to help you achieve the ideal dough consistency, ensuring that your tagliatelle turns out flawlessly every time.

Step-by-Step Guide to Making Homemade Tagliatelle Dough

Creating tagliatelle dough from scratch is a gratifying endeavor that allows you to connect with the very essence of the pasta. With each step, you'll develop an intuitive understanding of the ingredients, textures, and techniques that contribute to a remarkable tagliatelle experience.

Gather Your Ingredients: Assemble high-quality flour and eggs, ensuring their freshness and quality.

Create a Mound of Flour: On a clean work surface, form a mound of flour with a well in the center.

Add Eggs to the Well: Crack the eggs into the well, and gently whisk them with a fork, gradually incorporating the surrounding flour.

Mix to Form a Shaggy Dough: As you continue to whisk, the mixture will transition into a shaggy dough.

Knead the Dough: Begin kneading the dough, using the heels of your palms to push and fold it. This process develops gluten and creates elasticity.

Achieve a Smooth Texture: Knead until the dough becomes smooth and cohesive, about 10-15 minutes.

Rest the Dough: Wrap the dough in plastic wrap and let it rest for at least 30 minutes, allowing the gluten to relax.

Rolling the Dough: Flatten the rested dough with a rolling pin, then use a pasta machine to gradually thin it out.

Cutting the Dough: Feed the thin dough through the pasta machine's cutting attachment or use a knife to create elegant tagliatelle ribbons.

Drying or Cooking: If desired, hang the freshly cut tagliatelle on a drying rack or cook it immediately in a pot of boiling water until al dente.

Tips for Achieving the Ideal Dough Consistency

Achieving the perfect tagliatelle dough consistency is a blend of technique, intuition, and experience. These tips will guide you toward creating a dough that's pliable, manageable, and ready to transform into delectable pasta.

Flour Gradually: Incorporate the flour into the eggs slowly, adjusting as needed to achieve the desired consistency.

Texture Awareness: Pay attention to the dough's texture as you knead. It should transform from rough and uneven to smooth and supple.

Rest and Relax: Allowing the dough to rest is essential. It relaxes the gluten and makes the dough easier to work with.

Consistency Check: Aim for a dough that is neither too sticky nor too dry. It should be slightly tacky to the touch.

Adjust as You Go: Depending on factors like humidity and flour type, you may need to make minor adjustments to achieve the perfect dough.

Practice Makes Perfect: Like any culinary art, mastering tagliatelle dough takes practice. Don't be discouraged by initial attempts; each one brings you closer to perfection.

With dedication and practice, you'll soon develop an intuitive feel for the tagliatelle dough, creating a foundation that allows you to explore the myriad possibilities of pasta-making. As you proceed on your culinary journey, keep in mind that the mastery of tagliatelle dough is not just a skill but a rewarding and satisfying experience that brings you closer to the heart of Italian gastronomy.

Chapter 4: Classic Tagliatelle Recipes

In this chapter, we pay homage to the timeless allure of classic tagliatelle recipes. These dishes have stood the test of time, offering comfort, flavor, and a connection to tradition. Let's dive into the preparation of three iconic tagliatelle dishes: Traditional Tagliatelle Alfredo, Creamy Carbonara with Tagliatelle, and Bolognese Tagliatelle.

Traditional Tagliatelle Alfredo

Tagliatelle al Burro all'Alfredo is a celebrated Roman dish that marries simplicity with indulgence, creating a velvety, buttery sauce that clings luxuriously to each strand of tagliatelle.

Ingredients:

- Fresh tagliatelle pasta
- 1 cup unsalted butter, softened
- 1 cup heavy cream
- 1 cup freshly grated Parmesan cheese
- Salt and freshly ground black pepper, to taste
- Chopped parsley, for garnish

Instructions:

A. Cook the tagliatelle in salted boiling water until al dente. Drain and set aside.
B. In a saucepan over low heat, melt the butter and cream together, stirring until well combined.
C. Gradually whisk in the Parmesan cheese until the sauce is smooth and creamy. Season with salt and pepper.
D. Toss the cooked tagliatelle in the Alfredo sauce until well coated.

E. Serve immediately, garnished with chopped parsley and additional Parmesan cheese, if desired.

Creamy Carbonara with Tagliatelle

Tagliatelle alla Carbonara captures the essence of Roman cuisine with its rich, creamy sauce featuring pancetta, eggs, and Pecorino Romano cheese.

Ingredients:

- Fresh tagliatelle pasta
- 200g pancetta or guanciale, diced
- 3 large eggs
- 1 cup freshly grated Pecorino Romano cheese
- Freshly ground black pepper, to taste
- Chopped fresh parsley, for garnish

Instructions:

A. Cook the tagliatelle in salted boiling water until al dente. Reserve some pasta water and drain.
B. In a skillet, cook the diced pancetta or guanciale until crispy. Remove from heat.
C. In a bowl, whisk together the eggs, grated Pecorino Romano cheese, and a generous amount of black pepper.
D. Toss the cooked tagliatelle and pancetta in the egg mixture. Add a splash of pasta water to create a creamy sauce.
E. Serve immediately, garnished with chopped parsley.

Bolognese Tagliatelle

Tagliatelle al Ragù is a hearty dish that hails from Bologna, the birthplace of tagliatelle. The rich meat sauce coats the tagliatelle, creating a satisfying and comforting meal.

Ingredients:

- Fresh tagliatelle pasta
- 300g ground beef or a combination of beef and pork
- 1 onion, finely chopped
- 2 cloves garlic, minced
- 1 carrot, finely chopped
- 1 celery stalk, finely chopped
- 1 can (400g) crushed tomatoes
- 1/2 cup red wine
- Salt and freshly ground black pepper, to taste
- Freshly grated Parmesan cheese, for serving

Instructions:

A. Cook the tagliatelle in salted boiling water until al dente. Drain and set aside.
B. In a large skillet, brown the ground meat over medium heat. Drain excess fat.
C. Add the chopped onion, garlic, carrot, and celery to the skillet. Sauté until the vegetables are tender.
D. Pour in the red wine and cook until it reduces by half.
E. Stir in the crushed tomatoes and season with salt and black pepper. Simmer the sauce for about 20-30 minutes.
F. Toss the cooked tagliatelle in the Bolognese sauce until well coated.
G. Serve with freshly grated Parmesan cheese on top.

These classic tagliatelle recipes invite you to savor the rich history and flavors of Italian cuisine. With each forkful, you'll experience the comfort and satisfaction that these timeless dishes bring to the table.

Chapter 5: Fresh and Light Tagliatelle Dishes

In this chapter, we explore the lighter side of tagliatelle, where vibrant flavors and wholesome ingredients come together to create refreshing and satisfying dishes. Embrace the zest of Lemon and Herb Tagliatelle, delight in the richness of Spinach and Ricotta Stuffed Tagliatelle, and experience the Mediterranean essence of Tagliatelle Salad.

Lemon and Herb Tagliatelle

Lemon and Herb Tagliatelle is a celebration of bright flavors and fragrant herbs that invigorate the palate. This dish captures the essence of a sunny day with its refreshing and zesty profile.

Ingredients:

- Fresh tagliatelle pasta
- Zest and juice of 1 lemon
- 2 tablespoons extra-virgin olive oil
- Fresh mixed herbs (such as basil, parsley, and thyme), chopped
- Salt and freshly ground black pepper, to taste
- Grated Parmesan cheese, for serving

Instructions:

A. Cook the tagliatelle in salted boiling water until al dente. Drain and set aside.
B. In a bowl, whisk together the lemon zest, lemon juice, and olive oil.
C. Toss the cooked tagliatelle in the lemon and herb mixture until well coated.
D. Stir in the chopped fresh herbs and season with salt and black

pepper.

E. Serve immediately, garnished with grated Parmesan cheese.

Spinach and Ricotta Stuffed Tagliatelle

Spinach and Ricotta Stuffed Tagliatelle offers a delightful blend of creamy ricotta, tender spinach, and delicate pasta. This dish showcases the artistry of stuffed pasta while maintaining a light and wholesome character.

Ingredients:

- Fresh tagliatelle pasta
- 200g fresh spinach, blanched and chopped
- 250g ricotta cheese
- 1 egg
- 1/2 cup grated Parmesan cheese
- Salt and freshly ground black pepper, to taste
- Marinara sauce, for serving

Instructions:

A. Cook the tagliatelle in salted boiling water until al dente. Drain and set aside.
B. In a bowl, combine the blanched spinach, ricotta cheese, egg, grated Parmesan cheese, salt, and black pepper.
C. Lay out a sheet of tagliatelle and place small spoonfuls of the spinach and ricotta mixture along the length of the pasta.
D. Roll up the tagliatelle to encase the filling, creating stuffed pasta rolls.
E. Place the stuffed tagliatelle rolls in a baking dish and top with marinara sauce.

F. Bake in a preheated oven until heated through and the cheese is melted.

G. Serve warm, garnished with additional grated Parmesan cheese.

Mediterranean-Inspired Tagliatelle Salad

Tagliatelle Salad takes you on a journey to the Mediterranean coast, where fresh produce and bold flavors come together in a vibrant and satisfying dish.

Ingredients:

- Fresh tagliatelle pasta
- Cherry tomatoes, halved
- Cucumber, diced
- Kalamata olives, pitted and halved
- Red onion, thinly sliced
- Feta cheese, crumbled
- Fresh basil leaves, torn
- Extra-virgin olive oil
- Red wine vinegar
- Salt and freshly ground black pepper, to taste

Instructions:

A. Cook the tagliatelle in salted boiling water until al dente. Drain and set aside.

B. In a large bowl, combine the cooked tagliatelle, cherry tomatoes, cucumber, Kalamata olives, red onion, and feta cheese.

C. Drizzle with extra-virgin olive oil and a splash of red wine vinegar.
D. Toss the ingredients until well combined. Season with salt and black pepper.
E. Garnish with torn fresh basil leaves.
F. Serve as a refreshing and satisfying tagliatelle salad.

These fresh and light tagliatelle dishes offer a delightful departure from the ordinary, inviting you to embrace the flavors of herbs, vegetables, and cheeses that create a harmonious and invigorating culinary experience. Whether you're craving a zesty citrus kick, the comfort of stuffed pasta, or the vibrant essence of Mediterranean ingredients, these recipes have you covered.

Chapter 6: Gourmet Tagliatelle Creations

Indulge in the opulent world of gourmet tagliatelle creations. In this chapter, we present three sumptuous dishes that elevate tagliatelle to new heights of extravagance and refinement. Immerse yourself in the decadence of Truffle-Infused Tagliatelle, experience the luxurious pairing of Lobster and Champagne Tagliatelle, and savor the earthy elegance of Wild Mushroom and Thyme Tagliatelle.

Truffle-Infused Tagliatelle

Truffle-Infused Tagliatelle is a celebration of one of the culinary world's most coveted ingredients. The earthy aroma and delicate flavor of truffles elevate this dish to a level of unparalleled luxury.

Ingredients:

- Fresh tagliatelle pasta
- Truffle oil or fresh truffles, thinly sliced
- 1/4 cup heavy cream
- Grated Parmesan cheese
- Salt and freshly ground black pepper, to taste
- Fresh chives or parsley, chopped (for garnish)

Instructions:

1. Cook the tagliatelle in salted boiling water until al dente. Drain and set aside.
2. In a skillet, gently warm the truffle oil or fresh truffle slices over low heat.
3. Pour in the heavy cream and stir to combine. Allow the flavors to meld without boiling.
4. Toss the cooked tagliatelle in the truffle-infused cream sauce until well coated.

5. Season with salt and black pepper, then sprinkle with grated Parmesan cheese.
6. Serve immediately, garnished with chopped fresh chives or parsley.

Lobster and Champagne Tagliatelle

Lobster and Champagne Tagliatelle is a luxurious pairing that marries succulent lobster meat with the effervescence of champagne, resulting in an unforgettable gourmet experience.

Ingredients:

- Fresh tagliatelle pasta
- 2 lobster tails, cooked and meat removed
- 1 cup champagne or sparkling wine
- 1 shallot, finely chopped
- 1/2 cup heavy cream
- Fresh chives, chopped
- Salt and freshly ground black pepper, to taste

Instructions:

1. Cook the tagliatelle in salted boiling water until al dente. Drain and set aside.
2. In a saucepan, sauté the chopped shallot until translucent.
3. Pour in the champagne and simmer until it reduces by half.
4. Add the heavy cream and continue to simmer until the sauce thickens slightly.
5. Gently fold in the cooked lobster meat and heat through.
6. Toss the cooked tagliatelle in the lobster and champagne sauce until well combined.

7. Season with salt and black pepper, then garnish with chopped fresh chives.
8. Serve as a luxurious and elegant tagliatelle dish.

Wild Mushroom and Thyme Tagliatelle

Wild Mushroom and Thyme Tagliatelle celebrates the earthy richness of wild mushrooms, complemented by the aromatic notes of fresh thyme. This dish transports you to a forest of flavors.

Ingredients:

- Fresh tagliatelle pasta
- Assorted wild mushrooms (such as chanterelles, porcini, or shiitake), cleaned and sliced
- 2 cloves garlic, minced
- Fresh thyme leaves, chopped
- 1/4 cup dry white wine
- 1/4 cup chicken or vegetable broth
- Heavy cream (optional)
- Salt and freshly ground black pepper, to taste
- Grated Parmesan cheese, for serving

Instructions:

1. Cook the tagliatelle in salted boiling water until al dente. Drain and set aside.
2. In a skillet, sauté the minced garlic until fragrant.
3. Add the sliced wild mushrooms and cook until they release their moisture and become tender.
4. Pour in the white wine and cook until it reduces by half.
5. Add the chicken or vegetable broth and chopped fresh thyme.

Simmer for a few minutes.

6. If desired, add a splash of heavy cream for extra richness.

7. Toss the cooked tagliatelle in the wild mushroom and thyme sauce until well coated.

8. Season with salt and black pepper, and serve with grated Parmesan cheese.

These gourmet tagliatelle creations invite you to indulge in the luxurious world of fine ingredients and exquisite flavors. From the aromatic allure of truffles to the delicate pairing of lobster and champagne, each dish presents a symphony of tastes that will elevate your tagliatelle experience to a truly gourmet level.

Chapter 7: Sauces that Elevate Tagliatelle

A well-crafted sauce has the power to transform tagliatelle into a culinary masterpiece. In this chapter, we explore three exquisite sauces that elevate the flavors and textures of tagliatelle. Discover the art of creating Homemade Marinara Sauce, embrace the vibrant notes of Pesto Perfection with Tagliatelle, and savor the richness of Creamy Gorgonzola and Walnut Sauce.

Homemade Marinara Sauce

Homemade Marinara Sauce is a timeless classic that enhances the natural flavors of tagliatelle. This versatile sauce is the perfect canvas for your culinary creativity.

Ingredients:

- Fresh tagliatelle pasta
- 2 cans (14 oz each) crushed tomatoes
- 3 cloves garlic, minced
- 1/4 cup extra-virgin olive oil
- Fresh basil leaves, torn
- Crushed red pepper flakes, to taste
- Salt and freshly ground black pepper, to taste

Instructions:

1. Cook the tagliatelle in salted boiling water until al dente. Drain and set aside.
2. In a saucepan, heat the olive oil over medium heat. Add the minced garlic and sauté until fragrant.
3. Pour in the crushed tomatoes and bring the sauce to a simmer.
4. Season with salt, black pepper, and crushed red pepper flakes.
5. Let the sauce simmer for about 20-30 minutes, allowing the flavors to meld.

6. Toss the cooked tagliatelle in the homemade marinara sauce until well coated.
7. Serve immediately, garnished with torn fresh basil leaves.

Pesto Perfection with Tagliatelle

Pesto Perfection with Tagliatelle celebrates the vibrant flavors of fresh basil, pine nuts, and Parmesan cheese. This sauce adds a burst of color and a hint of nuttiness to your tagliatelle.

Ingredients:

- Fresh tagliatelle pasta
- 2 cups fresh basil leaves
- 1/2 cup pine nuts, toasted
- 1/2 cup grated Parmesan cheese
- 2 cloves garlic, minced
- 1/2 cup extra-virgin olive oil
- Salt and freshly ground black pepper, to taste

Instructions:

1. Cook the tagliatelle in salted boiling water until al dente. Drain and set aside.
2. In a food processor, combine the fresh basil, toasted pine nuts, grated Parmesan cheese, and minced garlic.
3. With the food processor running, gradually drizzle in the olive oil until a smooth pesto forms.
4. Season with salt and black pepper.
5. Toss the cooked tagliatelle in the pesto sauce until well coated.
6. Serve immediately, optionally garnished with additional grated Parmesan cheese.

Creamy Gorgonzola and Walnut Sauce

Creamy Gorgonzola and Walnut Sauce introduces a decadent and harmonious combination of rich gorgonzola cheese and toasted walnuts, creating a luscious sauce that envelops each strand of tagliatelle.

Ingredients:

- Fresh tagliatelle pasta
- 1 cup heavy cream
- 1 cup crumbled gorgonzola cheese
- 1/2 cup toasted walnuts, chopped
- Fresh parsley, chopped (for garnish)
- Salt and freshly ground black pepper, to taste

Instructions:

1. Cook the tagliatelle in salted boiling water until al dente. Drain and set aside.
2. In a saucepan, heat the heavy cream over medium heat until it starts to simmer.
3. Gradually add the crumbled gorgonzola cheese, stirring until melted and smooth.
4. Stir in the toasted chopped walnuts and season with salt and black pepper.
5. Toss the cooked tagliatelle in the creamy gorgonzola and walnut sauce until well coated.
6. Serve immediately, garnished with chopped fresh parsley.

These exquisite sauces have the ability to transform tagliatelle into a symphony of flavors and textures. Whether you're drawn to the comforting embrace of marinara, the vibrant essence of pesto, or the indulgent richness of gorgonzola and walnut, each sauce showcases the art of culinary balance and harmony.

Chapter 8: Seafood Lovers' Tagliatelle

For those who appreciate the bounty of the sea, this chapter is a seafood lover's paradise. Immerse yourself in the exquisite flavors of Shrimp Scampi Tagliatelle, indulge in the luxurious combination of Scallop and Saffron Tagliatelle, and savor the delicate harmony of Smoked Salmon and Dill Tagliatelle.

Shrimp Scampi Tagliatelle

Shrimp Scampi Tagliatelle is a symphony of succulent shrimp, garlic, and white wine, creating a dish that showcases the delicate sweetness of seafood.

Ingredients:

- Fresh tagliatelle pasta
- Large shrimp, peeled and deveined
- 4 cloves garlic, minced
- 1/4 cup dry white wine
- Juice of 1 lemon
- Fresh parsley, chopped
- Red pepper flakes, to taste
- Salt and freshly ground black pepper, to taste

Instructions:

1. Cook the tagliatelle in salted boiling water until al dente. Drain and set aside.
2. In a skillet, sauté the minced garlic in olive oil until fragrant.
3. Add the shrimp and cook until they turn pink and opaque.
4. Pour in the white wine and lemon juice. Simmer for a few minutes.
5. Season with salt, black pepper, and red pepper flakes.
6. Toss the cooked tagliatelle in the shrimp scampi sauce until well

coated.

7. Serve immediately, garnished with chopped fresh parsley.

Scallop and Saffron Tagliatelle

Scallop and Saffron Tagliatelle is a marriage of delicate scallops and the golden allure of saffron, creating a dish that's as visually captivating as it is flavorful.

Ingredients:

- Fresh tagliatelle pasta
- Large sea scallops
- 1/4 teaspoon saffron threads, soaked in warm water
- 1/4 cup dry white wine
- 1/2 cup heavy cream
- Fresh chives, chopped
- Salt and freshly ground black pepper, to taste

Instructions:

1. Cook the tagliatelle in salted boiling water until al dente. Drain and set aside.
2. In a skillet, sear the scallops until golden and cooked through. Set aside.
3. In the same skillet, pour in the white wine and bring it to a simmer.
4. Add the soaked saffron threads and heavy cream. Simmer until the sauce thickens slightly.
5. Season with salt and black pepper.
6. Toss the cooked tagliatelle in the saffron cream sauce until well coated.

7. Serve the tagliatelle topped with seared scallops and chopped
    fresh chives.

Smoked Salmon and Dill Tagliatelle

Smoked Salmon and Dill Tagliatelle brings together the luxurious flavor of smoked salmon with the herbaceous brightness of dill, creating a dish that's elegant and full of character.

Ingredients:

- Fresh tagliatelle pasta
- Smoked salmon, thinly sliced
- 1/2 cup heavy cream
- Fresh dill, chopped
- Juice of 1 lemon
- Salt and freshly ground black pepper, to taste

Instructions:

1. Cook the tagliatelle in salted boiling water until al dente. Drain and set aside.
2. In a saucepan, heat the heavy cream over medium heat until it starts to simmer.
3. Add the smoked salmon slices and chopped fresh dill. Simmer for a few minutes.
4. Season with salt, black pepper, and lemon juice.
5. Toss the cooked tagliatelle in the creamy smoked salmon and dill sauce until well coated.
6. Serve immediately, garnished with additional chopped fresh dill.

These seafood-inspired tagliatelle dishes allow you to indulge in the ocean's bounty while embracing the art of culinary creativity. Whether you're drawn to the vibrant flavors of shrimp scampi, the luxurious elegance of scallops and saffron, or the delicate harmony of smoked salmon and dill, each dish is a testament to the versatility of tagliatelle and the treasures of the sea.

Chapter 9: Comforting Tagliatelle Casseroles

In this chapter, we delve into the realm of comforting tagliatelle casseroles, where rich flavors and wholesome ingredients come together to create hearty and satisfying dishes. Experience the warmth of Chicken and Broccoli Tagliatelle Bake, indulge in the robustness of Beef and Mushroom Tagliatelle Casserole, and delight in the creamy goodness of Creamy Spinach and Artichoke Tagliatelle.

Chicken and Broccoli Tagliatelle Bake

Chicken and Broccoli Tagliatelle Bake combines tender chicken, vibrant broccoli, and tagliatelle in a creamy sauce, all baked to golden perfection for a comforting and wholesome meal.

Ingredients:

- Fresh tagliatelle pasta
- Boneless, skinless chicken breasts, cooked and cubed
- Fresh broccoli florets, blanched
- 1 cup heavy cream
- 1 cup chicken broth
- Grated Parmesan cheese
- Garlic powder, onion powder, salt, and black pepper, to taste
- Breadcrumbs (optional, for topping)
- Fresh parsley, chopped (for garnish)

Instructions:

1. Cook the tagliatelle in salted boiling water until al dente. Drain and set aside.
2. In a saucepan, combine the heavy cream and chicken broth. Bring to a simmer.

3. Season the cream mixture with garlic powder, onion powder, salt, and black pepper.
4. Stir in the cooked chicken cubes and blanched broccoli florets.
5. Toss the cooked tagliatelle in the creamy chicken and broccoli mixture until well combined.
6. Transfer the mixture to a baking dish and sprinkle with grated Parmesan cheese.
7. If desired, top with breadcrumbs for a crispy texture.
8. Bake in a preheated oven until the top is golden and bubbly.
9. Garnish with chopped fresh parsley before serving.

Beef and Mushroom Tagliatelle Casserole

Beef and Mushroom Tagliatelle Casserole embraces the heartiness of beef and the earthy flavors of mushrooms, creating a casserole that's a true comfort food delight.

Ingredients:

- Fresh tagliatelle pasta
- Ground beef
- Assorted mushrooms (such as cremini or button), sliced
- 1 onion, chopped
- 2 cloves garlic, minced
- 1 cup beef broth
- 1 cup heavy cream
- Worcestershire sauce
- Salt, black pepper, and thyme, to taste
- Grated Parmesan cheese
- Breadcrumbs (optional, for topping)
- Fresh parsley, chopped (for garnish)

Instructions:

1. Cook the tagliatelle in salted boiling water until al dente. Drain and set aside.
2. In a skillet, brown the ground beef. Drain excess fat.
3. Add the chopped onion, minced garlic, and sliced mushrooms. Sauté until tender.
4. Pour in the beef broth and simmer for a few minutes.
5. Stir in the heavy cream and a dash of Worcestershire sauce.
6. Season with salt, black pepper, and thyme.
7. Toss the cooked tagliatelle in the beef and mushroom mixture until well coated.
8. Transfer the mixture to a baking dish and sprinkle with grated

Parmesan cheese.

9. If desired, top with breadcrumbs for a crispy texture.
10. Bake in a preheated oven until the top is golden and bubbly.
11. Garnish with chopped fresh parsley before serving.

Creamy Spinach and Artichoke Tagliatelle

Creamy Spinach and Artichoke Tagliatelle combines the earthy flavors of spinach and the tangy goodness of artichokes in a lusciously creamy sauce.

Ingredients:

- Fresh tagliatelle pasta
- Fresh spinach, chopped
- Canned artichoke hearts, drained and chopped
- 1 cup heavy cream
- 1/2 cup grated Parmesan cheese
- 2 cloves garlic, minced
- Nutmeg, to taste
- Salt and black pepper, to taste

Instructions:

1. Cook the tagliatelle in salted boiling water until al dente. Drain and set aside.
2. In a skillet, sauté the minced garlic until fragrant.
3. Add the chopped spinach and artichoke hearts. Sauté until wilted.
4. Pour in the heavy cream and simmer for a few minutes.
5. Stir in the grated Parmesan cheese and a pinch of nutmeg.
6. Season with salt and black pepper.

7. Toss the cooked tagliatelle in the creamy spinach and artichoke sauce until well coated.
8. Serve immediately, optionally garnished with additional grated Parmesan cheese.

These comforting tagliatelle casseroles invite you to savor the heartwarming flavors of home-cooked goodness. Whether you're craving the tender combination of chicken and broccoli, the robust satisfaction of beef and mushrooms, or the creamy indulgence of spinach and artichoke, each casserole offers a satisfying embrace that warms both body and soul.

Chapter 10: International Twists on Tagliatelle

Embark on a global culinary adventure as we explore three captivating international twists on tagliatelle. From the aromatic allure of Thai-Inspired Peanut Tagliatelle to the vibrant spices of Indian Masala Tagliatelle and the tantalizing flavors of Chinese-Style Sesame Ginger Tagliatelle, these dishes showcase the fusion of cultures and tastes that make the world's cuisine so rich and diverse.

Thai-Inspired Peanut Tagliatelle

Thai-Inspired Peanut Tagliatelle captures the essence of Thai cuisine with its creamy peanut sauce and a hint of spice. This dish brings together the flavors of Southeast Asia and Italy in a harmonious fusion.

Ingredients:

- Fresh tagliatelle pasta
- Creamy peanut butter
- Coconut milk
- Soy sauce
- Lime juice
- Red curry paste (optional, for heat)
- Chopped peanuts, for garnish
- Fresh cilantro, chopped (for garnish)

Instructions:

1. Cook the tagliatelle in salted boiling water until al dente. Drain and set aside.
2. In a saucepan, combine creamy peanut butter, coconut milk, soy sauce, lime juice, and red curry paste (if using). Simmer until well combined and heated through.

3. Toss the cooked tagliatelle in the Thai-inspired peanut sauce until well coated.

4. Serve immediately, garnished with chopped peanuts and fresh cilantro.

Indian Masala Tagliatelle

Indian Masala Tagliatelle marries the aromatic spices of Indian cuisine with the comforting appeal of tagliatelle, creating a dish that's both familiar and exotic.

Ingredients:

- Fresh tagliatelle pasta
- Onions, finely chopped
- Tomatoes, chopped
- Ginger and garlic paste
- Garam masala, turmeric, cumin, and coriander powder
- Fresh cilantro, chopped (for garnish)

Instructions:

1. Cook the tagliatelle in salted boiling water until al dente. Drain and set aside.

2. In a skillet, sauté the finely chopped onions until golden.

3. Add the ginger and garlic paste and sauté until fragrant.

4. Stir in the chopped tomatoes and cook until they break down.

5. Add garam masala, turmeric, cumin, and coriander powder. Adjust spices to taste.

6. Toss the cooked tagliatelle in the Indian masala sauce until well coated.

7. Serve immediately, garnished with chopped fresh cilantro.

Chinese-Style Sesame Ginger Tagliatelle

Chinese-Style Sesame Ginger Tagliatelle brings the bold flavors of Chinese cuisine to the forefront, with a delectable combination of sesame and ginger that's both comforting and invigorating.

Ingredients:

- Fresh tagliatelle pasta
- Sesame oil
- Fresh ginger, grated
- Soy sauce
- Rice vinegar
- Honey or brown sugar
- Toasted sesame seeds, for garnish
- Sliced green onions, for garnish

Instructions:

1. Cook the tagliatelle in salted boiling water until al dente. Drain and set aside.
2. In a bowl, whisk together sesame oil, grated fresh ginger, soy sauce, rice vinegar, and honey or brown sugar to create a balanced dressing.
3. Toss the cooked tagliatelle in the Chinese-style sesame ginger dressing until well coated.
4. Serve immediately, garnished with toasted sesame seeds and sliced green onions.

These international twists on tagliatelle offer a passport to diverse and captivating flavors from around the world. Whether you're drawn to the creamy allure of Thai peanut sauce, the aromatic spices of Indian masala, or the bold sesame ginger notes of Chinese cuisine, each dish brings an exciting fusion of cultures to your tagliatelle experience.

Chapter 11: Vegan and Vegetarian Tagliatelle Delights

Explore the world of plant-based cuisine with these three delectable vegan and vegetarian tagliatelle delights. From the lusciousness of Vegan Cashew Cream Tagliatelle to the hearty goodness of Roasted Vegetable Tagliatelle and the Mediterranean-inspired Eggplant and Sun-Dried Tomato Tagliatelle, these dishes showcase the diverse and satisfying flavors of plant-based ingredients.

Vegan Cashew Cream Tagliatelle

Vegan Cashew Cream Tagliatelle is a creamy and indulgent pasta dish that doesn't compromise on flavor. The cashew-based cream sauce brings richness to every bite.

Ingredients:

- Fresh tagliatelle pasta
- Raw cashews, soaked and drained
- Nutritional yeast
- Garlic powder
- Lemon juice
- Vegetable broth
- Salt and freshly ground black pepper, to taste
- Fresh parsley, chopped (for garnish)

Instructions:

1. Cook the tagliatelle in salted boiling water until al dente. Drain

and set aside.

2. In a blender, combine soaked cashews, nutritional yeast, garlic powder, lemon juice, and vegetable broth. Blend until smooth and creamy.

3. Season with salt and black pepper to taste.

4. Toss the cooked tagliatelle in the vegan cashew cream sauce until well coated.

5. Serve immediately, garnished with chopped fresh parsley.

Roasted Vegetable Tagliatelle

Roasted Vegetable Tagliatelle celebrates the natural flavors of seasonal vegetables, roasted to perfection and tossed with tagliatelle for a satisfying and wholesome meal.

Ingredients:

- Fresh tagliatelle pasta
- Assorted vegetables (such as bell peppers, zucchini, cherry tomatoes, and red onion), chopped
- Olive oil
- Fresh thyme leaves
- Balsamic vinegar
- Salt and freshly ground black pepper, to taste
- Fresh basil, torn (for garnish)

Instructions:

1. Cook the tagliatelle in salted boiling water until al dente. Drain and set aside.
2. Toss the chopped vegetables in olive oil, fresh thyme leaves, balsamic vinegar, salt, and black pepper.
3. Roast the vegetables in a preheated oven until tender and slightly caramelized.
4. Toss the cooked tagliatelle with the roasted vegetables until well combined.
5. Serve immediately, garnished with torn fresh basil.

Eggplant and Sun-Dried Tomato Tagliatelle

Eggplant and Sun-Dried Tomato Tagliatelle offers a burst of Mediterranean flavors with tender eggplant and the tangy sweetness of sun-dried tomatoes.

Ingredients:

- Fresh tagliatelle pasta
- Eggplant, cubed
- Sun-dried tomatoes, chopped
- Kalamata olives, pitted and chopped
- Fresh basil, chopped
- Lemon zest
- Olive oil
- Salt and freshly ground black pepper, to taste

Instructions:

1. Cook the tagliatelle in salted boiling water until al dente. Drain and set aside.
2. In a skillet, sauté the cubed eggplant in olive oil until golden and tender.
3. Stir in the chopped sun-dried tomatoes and Kalamata olives.
4. Toss the cooked tagliatelle with the eggplant and sun-dried tomato mixture until well combined.
5. Season with salt and black pepper.
6. Serve immediately, garnished with chopped fresh basil and lemon zest.

These vegan and vegetarian tagliatelle delights showcase the beauty and variety of plant-based ingredients. Whether you're indulging in the creamy richness of cashew cream, savoring the natural flavors of roasted vegetables, or embracing the Mediterranean charm of eggplant and sun-dried tomatoes, each dish brings a unique and satisfying twist to your tagliatelle experience.

Chapter 12: Quick and Easy Tagliatelle Meals

For those busy days when time is of the essence, these three quick and easy tagliatelle meals will come to your rescue. From the simplicity of a One-Pan Garlic Butter Tagliatelle to the freshness of Tagliatelle Primavera and the flavorful Speedy Weeknight Sausage and Pepper Tagliatelle, these recipes offer convenience without compromising on taste.

One-Pan Garlic Butter Tagliatelle

One-Pan Garlic Butter Tagliatelle is the epitome of quick and easy comfort. With minimal ingredients and just one pan, you'll have a satisfying meal on the table in no time.

Ingredients:

- Fresh tagliatelle pasta
- Butter
- Garlic, minced
- Fresh parsley, chopped
- Grated Parmesan cheese
- Salt and freshly ground black pepper, to taste

Instructions:

1. Cook the tagliatelle in salted boiling water until al dente. Drain and set aside.
2. In the same pan, melt butter over medium heat.
3. Add minced garlic and sauté until fragrant.
4. Toss the cooked tagliatelle in the garlic butter sauce until well coated.
5. Season with salt and black pepper.

6. Serve immediately, garnished with chopped fresh parsley and grated Parmesan cheese.

Tagliatelle Primavera

Tagliatelle Primavera is a celebration of fresh, seasonal vegetables. This dish is a burst of color and flavor that's perfect for a quick and vibrant meal.

Ingredients:

- Fresh tagliatelle pasta
- Assorted vegetables (such as bell peppers, zucchini, cherry tomatoes, and carrots), sliced or diced
- Olive oil
- Fresh basil or parsley, chopped
- Lemon juice
- Salt and freshly ground black pepper, to taste

Instructions:

1. Cook the tagliatelle in salted boiling water until al dente. Drain and set aside.
2. In a skillet, sauté the assorted vegetables in olive oil until tender-crisp.
3. Toss the cooked tagliatelle with the sautéed vegetables until well combined.
4. Drizzle with fresh lemon juice and season with salt and black pepper.
5. Serve immediately, garnished with chopped fresh basil or parsley.

Speedy Weeknight Sausage and Pepper Tagliatelle

Speedy Weeknight Sausage and Pepper Tagliatelle combines savory sausage and colorful bell peppers for a satisfying and quick meal that's perfect for busy evenings.

Ingredients:

- Fresh tagliatelle pasta
- Italian sausage, casings removed
- Bell peppers (assorted colors), sliced
- Onion, sliced
- Olive oil
- Italian seasoning
- Crushed red pepper flakes (optional, for heat)
- Salt and freshly ground black pepper, to taste

Instructions:

1. Cook the tagliatelle in salted boiling water until al dente. Drain and set aside.
2. In a skillet, cook the Italian sausage, breaking it apart with a spatula, until browned and cooked through. Remove from the pan and set aside.
3. In the same skillet, sauté the sliced bell peppers and onion in olive oil until tender.
4. Add the cooked sausage back to the skillet. Season with Italian seasoning and crushed red pepper flakes (if using). Cook for a few more minutes to combine flavors.
5. Toss the cooked tagliatelle with the sausage and pepper mixture until well coated.
6. Season with salt and black pepper.

7. Serve immediately as a hearty and flavorful weeknight meal.

These quick and easy tagliatelle meals are designed to save time without sacrificing taste. Whether you're craving the simplicity of garlic butter, the freshness of seasonal vegetables, or the savory goodness of sausage and peppers, these recipes ensure that you can enjoy a satisfying and delicious meal even on the busiest days.

Chapter 13: Fresh Homemade Sauces

Elevate your tagliatelle experience with the art of crafting delectable homemade sauces. In this chapter, we explore three enticing options: Roasted Red Pepper and Tomato Sauce, Creamy Basil and Pine Nut Sauce, and Caramelized Onion and Balsamic Reduction. These sauces are a testament to the magic that happens when simple, fresh ingredients come together to create unforgettable flavors.

Roasted Red Pepper and Tomato Sauce

Roasted Red Pepper and Tomato Sauce combines the smoky sweetness of roasted red peppers with the rich tanginess of tomatoes, resulting in a harmonious sauce that brings depth to your tagliatelle.

Ingredients:

- Fresh tagliatelle pasta
- Red bell peppers, roasted and peeled
- Tomatoes, peeled and chopped
- Onion, chopped
- Garlic, minced
- Olive oil
- Fresh basil, chopped
- Salt and freshly ground black pepper, to taste

Instructions:

1. Cook the tagliatelle in salted boiling water until al dente. Drain and set aside.
2. In a saucepan, sauté the chopped onion and minced garlic in olive oil until softened.
3. Add the roasted red peppers and chopped tomatoes. Simmer until the tomatoes break down and the flavors meld.
4. Blend the sauce until smooth using a blender or immersion

blender.

5. Return the sauce to the pan and season with salt and black pepper.

6. Toss the cooked tagliatelle in the roasted red pepper and tomato sauce until well coated.

7. Serve immediately, garnished with chopped fresh basil.

Creamy Basil and Pine Nut Sauce

Creamy Basil and Pine Nut Sauce combines the aromatic essence of fresh basil with the richness of pine nuts and cream, creating a luscious and indulgent sauce for your tagliatelle.

Ingredients:

- Fresh tagliatelle pasta
- Fresh basil leaves
- Pine nuts, toasted
- Garlic, minced
- Olive oil
- Heavy cream
- Grated Parmesan cheese
- Salt and freshly ground black pepper, to taste

Instructions:

1. Cook the tagliatelle in salted boiling water until al dente. Drain and set aside.

2. In a food processor, combine fresh basil leaves, toasted pine nuts, minced garlic, and olive oil. Blend until a smooth basil pesto forms.

3. In a saucepan, heat the heavy cream over medium heat until it starts to simmer.

4. Stir in the prepared basil pesto and grated Parmesan cheese until well combined.

5. Season with salt and black pepper to taste.
6. Toss the cooked tagliatelle in the creamy basil and pine nut sauce until well coated.
7. Serve immediately, optionally garnished with additional grated Parmesan cheese.

Caramelized Onion and Balsamic Reduction

Caramelized Onion and Balsamic Reduction offers a combination of sweet, savory, and tangy flavors, creating a unique and sophisticated sauce for your tagliatelle.

Ingredients:

- Fresh tagliatelle pasta
- Onions, thinly sliced
- Balsamic vinegar
- Brown sugar
- Olive oil
- Fresh thyme leaves, chopped
- Salt and freshly ground black pepper, to taste

Instructions:

1. Cook the tagliatelle in salted boiling water until al dente. Drain and set aside.
2. In a skillet, heat olive oil over medium-low heat. Add the thinly sliced onions and cook until caramelized and golden.
3. Stir in balsamic vinegar and brown sugar. Continue cooking until the mixture thickens and becomes a reduction.
4. Add chopped fresh thyme leaves and season with salt and black pepper.

5. Toss the cooked tagliatelle in the caramelized onion and balsamic reduction until well coated.
6. Serve immediately, optionally garnished with additional fresh thyme leaves.

These fresh homemade sauces showcase the art of transforming simple ingredients into exquisite flavors. Whether you're drawn to the smoky sweetness of roasted red pepper and tomato, the creamy indulgence of basil and pine nut, or the sophisticated balance of caramelized onion and balsamic reduction, each sauce invites you to savor the magic of culinary creativity.

Chapter 14: Tagliatelle for Special Occasions

Celebrate life's extraordinary moments with these luxurious and unforgettable tagliatelle dishes, specially crafted for special occasions. From the indulgence of Holiday Truffle and Herb Tagliatelle to the opulence of Anniversary Lobster Tagliatelle and the elegance of Champagne Cream Tagliatelle, these recipes are destined to create lasting memories and leave a lasting impression.

Holiday Truffle and Herb Tagliatelle

Holiday Truffle and Herb Tagliatelle embodies the essence of celebration with the exquisite flavors of truffle and fragrant herbs, making it the perfect centerpiece for festive gatherings.

Ingredients:

- Fresh tagliatelle pasta
- Truffle oil or truffle butter
- Mixed fresh herbs (such as thyme, rosemary, and sage), chopped
- Grated Parmesan cheese
- Salt and freshly ground black pepper, to taste

Instructions:

1. Cook the tagliatelle in salted boiling water until al dente. Drain and set aside.
2. Drizzle truffle oil or melt truffle butter in a skillet over low heat.
3. Toss the cooked tagliatelle in the truffle oil or butter until well coated.
4. Add the chopped mixed herbs and grated Parmesan cheese. Gently toss to combine.

5. Season with salt and black pepper to taste.
6. Serve immediately, garnished with additional grated Parmesan cheese.

Chapter 15: Artisanal Flavored Tagliatelle Variations

Embark on a journey of culinary artistry with these unique and vibrant artisanal flavored tagliatelle variations. From the stunning hue of Beetroot-Infused Tagliatelle to the intriguing depths of Squid Ink Tagliatelle and the golden allure of Saffron and Sun-Dried Tomato Tagliatelle, these recipes are a testament to the creativity and beauty that can be achieved in the kitchen.

Beetroot-Infused Tagliatelle

Beetroot-Infused Tagliatelle brings a burst of color to your plate, showcasing the natural beauty and earthy flavors of beetroots in every delicious strand.

Ingredients:

- Fresh tagliatelle pasta
- Beetroot puree (cooked and blended beetroot)
- Olive oil
- Fresh thyme leaves
- Salt and freshly ground black pepper, to taste

Instructions:

1. Cook the tagliatelle in salted boiling water until al dente. Drain and set aside.
2. In a skillet, warm olive oil over medium heat. Add the beetroot puree and fresh thyme leaves. Cook for a few minutes to combine flavors.
3. Toss the cooked tagliatelle in the beetroot-infused sauce until well coated.

4. Season with salt and black pepper to taste.
5. Serve immediately, optionally garnished with additional fresh thyme leaves.

Squid Ink Tagliatelle

Squid Ink Tagliatelle is a visually striking and bold variation, capturing the essence of the ocean with its distinct color and subtle briny flavor.

Ingredients:

- Fresh squid ink tagliatelle pasta
- Olive oil
- Garlic, minced
- Red pepper flakes, to taste
- Fresh parsley, chopped
- Salt and freshly ground black pepper, to taste

Instructions:

1. Cook the squid ink tagliatelle in salted boiling water until al dente. Drain and set aside.
2. In a skillet, sauté the minced garlic in olive oil until fragrant.
3. Add the cooked squid ink tagliatelle to the skillet. Toss to coat with the garlic-infused oil.
4. Season with red pepper flakes, salt, and black pepper to taste.
5. Serve immediately, garnished with chopped fresh parsley.

Chapter 16: Tagliatelle from Scratch: Advanced Techniques

Take your tagliatelle-making skills to the next level with advanced techniques that involve crafting colored and flavored pasta doughs, as well as creating rolled and filled tagliatelle variations. These intricate methods showcase your culinary expertise and allow you to create visually stunning and exceptionally flavorful tagliatelle dishes.

Colored and Flavored Pasta Doughs

Creating colored and flavored pasta doughs adds a delightful twist to your tagliatelle creations, transforming them into works of art that are as pleasing to the eye as they are to the palate.

Ingredients:

- Basic pasta dough ingredients (flour, eggs, salt)

For Colored Doughs:

- Natural food colorings (spinach for green, beetroot for red, turmeric for yellow, etc.)

For Flavored Doughs:

- Flavored powders or purees (spinach puree, tomato paste, squid ink, etc.)

Instructions:

1. Prepare the basic pasta dough by combining flour, eggs, and salt. Knead until smooth and elastic.
2. Divide the dough into portions for different colors or flavors

you want to create.

3. For colored doughs, incorporate natural food colorings into the dough while kneading, until the desired color is achieved. Add a little at a time to avoid making the dough too wet.

4. For flavored doughs, incorporate flavored powders or purees into the dough while kneading, ensuring even distribution.

5. Once the colored or flavored dough is well-mixed and smooth, cover and let it rest for about 30 minutes.

6. Roll out the colored or flavored dough to the desired thickness using a pasta machine or rolling pin.

7. Cut the rolled dough into tagliatelle strips using a pasta cutter or a knife.

8. Cook the tagliatelle in salted boiling water until al dente, then drain and serve with your favorite sauce.

Rolled and Filled Tagliatelle Variations

Creating rolled and filled tagliatelle variations adds a level of complexity and elegance to your pasta creations, perfect for showcasing your advanced culinary skills.

Ingredients:

- Fresh pasta dough
- Filling ingredients (such as ricotta cheese and spinach, mushroom duxelles, lobster meat, etc.)

Instructions:

1. Prepare a batch of fresh pasta dough.
2. Roll out the pasta dough into thin sheets using a pasta machine or rolling pin.
3. For rolled variations, cut the sheets into wide strips, then roll them into elegant cylinders. Slice the rolled cylinders into tagliatelle-width strips.

4. For filled variations, place small spoonfuls of your chosen filling along the pasta sheet, leaving space between each portion. Fold the pasta sheet over the filling and press gently to seal.
5. Cut the folded sheet into tagliatelle strips using a pasta cutter or knife.
6. Cook the rolled or filled tagliatelle in salted boiling water until al dente, then drain and serve with a complementary sauce.

Mastering colored and flavored pasta doughs, as well as rolled and filled tagliatelle variations, allows you to create visually stunning and incredibly delicious dishes that showcase your advanced culinary techniques. Whether you're crafting vibrant and aromatic doughs or experimenting with intricate fillings, these techniques open up a world of possibilities for creating tagliatelle dishes that are truly works of art.

Chapter 17: Gluten-Free Tagliatelle Options

Delight in the world of gluten-free tagliatelle with this chapter dedicated to crafting gluten-free tagliatelle dough and exploring a variety of flavorful gluten-free sauce options. These recipes ensure that individuals with gluten sensitivities or dietary preferences can still enjoy the exquisite taste and texture of tagliatelle.

Making Gluten-Free Tagliatelle Dough

Crafting gluten-free tagliatelle dough requires a blend of alternative flours and techniques to achieve a dough that is both pliable and delicious.

Ingredients:

- Gluten-free flour blend (such as rice flour, cornstarch, and tapioca flour)
- Xanthan gum (for binding)
- Eggs
- Water (as needed)
- Salt

Instructions:

1. In a mixing bowl, combine the gluten-free flour blend and xanthan gum.
2. Create a well in the center of the flour mixture and crack the eggs into it.
3. Gradually incorporate the flour into the eggs, mixing with a fork or your hands.
4. If the dough is too dry, add water, a little at a time, until the dough comes together.
5. Knead the dough until it is smooth and pliable, adding more

flour if needed to prevent sticking.

6. Let the dough rest for about 30 minutes before rolling and shaping into tagliatelle strips.

7. Roll out the dough into thin sheets using a pasta machine or rolling pin.

8. Cut the sheets into tagliatelle strips using a pasta cutter or knife.

9. Cook the gluten-free tagliatelle in salted boiling water until al dente, then drain and serve.

Gluten-Free Sauce Options

Pair your gluten-free tagliatelle with a variety of flavorful and satisfying gluten-free sauce options.

1. Classic Marinara Sauce:

Ingredients:

- Crushed tomatoes
- Olive oil
- Garlic, minced
- Dried oregano and basil
- Salt and freshly ground black pepper
- Fresh basil, chopped (for garnish)

Instructions:

1. In a saucepan, heat olive oil over medium heat. Add minced garlic and sauté until fragrant.

2. Add crushed tomatoes, dried oregano, dried basil, salt, and black pepper. Simmer until the sauce thickens.

3. Toss the cooked gluten-free tagliatelle in the marinara sauce until well coated.

4. Serve immediately, garnished with chopped fresh basil.

2. Creamy Avocado Pesto:
Ingredients:

- Fresh basil leaves
- Avocado
- Pine nuts
- Garlic, minced
- Lemon juice
- Olive oil
- Salt and freshly ground black pepper
- Grated Parmesan cheese (optional)

Instructions:

1. In a food processor, combine fresh basil leaves, avocado, pine nuts, minced garlic, lemon juice, and olive oil. Blend until smooth.
2. Season with salt and black pepper to taste. Add grated Parmesan cheese if desired.
3. Toss the cooked gluten-free tagliatelle in the creamy avocado pesto until well coated.
4. Serve immediately.

3. Creamy Mushroom Alfredo:
Ingredients:

- Assorted mushrooms (such as cremini, shiitake, and oyster), sliced
- Butter
- Heavy cream

- Garlic, minced
- Grated Parmesan cheese
- Fresh parsley, chopped (for garnish)
- Salt and freshly ground black pepper

Instructions:

1. In a skillet, melt butter over medium heat. Add sliced mushrooms and sauté until browned and tender.
2. Stir in minced garlic and cook until fragrant.
3. Pour in heavy cream and bring to a gentle simmer.
4. Add grated Parmesan cheese and stir until the sauce thickens.
5. Toss the cooked gluten-free tagliatelle in the creamy mushroom Alfredo sauce until well coated.
6. Season with salt and black pepper to taste.
7. Serve immediately, garnished with chopped fresh parsley.

These gluten-free tagliatelle options showcase the beauty of alternative flours and ingredients, allowing you to enjoy the flavors and textures of tagliatelle without gluten. Whether you're opting for a classic marinara, a creamy avocado pesto, or a luxurious mushroom Alfredo, these gluten-free sauce options are the perfect companions for your homemade gluten-free tagliatelle.

Chapter 18: Leftover Remix: Creative Tagliatelle Recipes

Don't let your leftover tagliatelle go to waste! This chapter is dedicated to turning those remnants into exciting new creations. From a Tagliatelle Frittata that's perfect for breakfast or brunch, to Tagliatelle-Stuffed Bell Peppers that make a delicious and unique main course, and a refreshing Tagliatelle Panzanella Salad that reinvents your leftovers into a delightful summer dish.

Tagliatelle Frittata

Tagliatelle Frittata transforms leftover tagliatelle into a hearty and flavorful breakfast or brunch dish that's perfect for using up those extra strands.

Ingredients:

- Leftover tagliatelle pasta
- Eggs
- Milk or cream
- Grated cheese (such as Parmesan or cheddar)
- Fresh herbs (such as parsley, thyme, or chives), chopped
- Salt and freshly ground black pepper

Instructions:

1. Preheat the oven to 350°F (175°C).
2. In a bowl, whisk together eggs, milk or cream, grated cheese, chopped fresh herbs, salt, and black pepper.
3. Add the leftover tagliatelle to the egg mixture and stir to combine.
4. Heat an oven-safe skillet over medium heat. Add a bit of oil or butter.

5. Pour the tagliatelle and egg mixture into the skillet and cook for a few minutes until the edges start to set.
6. Transfer the skillet to the preheated oven and bake for about 15-20 minutes, or until the frittata is set and slightly golden on top.
7. Slice and serve the tagliatelle frittata warm.

Tagliatelle-Stuffed Bell Peppers

Tagliatelle-Stuffed Bell Peppers is a creative way to transform leftover tagliatelle into a satisfying and visually appealing dish.

Ingredients:

- Leftover tagliatelle pasta
- Bell peppers, halved and seeds removed
- Tomato sauce
- Shredded mozzarella cheese
- Fresh basil, chopped (for garnish)
- Salt and freshly ground black pepper

Instructions

1. Preheat the oven to 375°F (190°C).
2. Mix the leftover tagliatelle with tomato sauce and a bit of shredded mozzarella cheese.
3. Stuff the halved bell peppers with the tagliatelle mixture.
4. Place the stuffed peppers in a baking dish.
5. Cover the peppers with aluminum foil and bake for about 20-25 minutes, or until the peppers are tender.
6. Remove the foil and sprinkle additional shredded mozzarella cheese on top of each pepper.
7. Return the peppers to the oven and bake for an additional 5-7 minutes, or until the cheese is melted and bubbly.

8. Garnish with chopped fresh basil before serving.

Tagliatelle Panzanella Salad
Tagliatelle Panzanella Salad breathes new life into leftover tagliatelle by turning it into a refreshing and vibrant summer salad.
Ingredients:

- Leftover tagliatelle pasta
- Cherry tomatoes, halved
- Cucumber, diced
- Red onion, thinly sliced
- Fresh basil leaves, torn
- Kalamata olives, pitted and halved
- Olive oil
- Balsamic vinegar
- Salt and freshly ground black pepper

Instructions:

1. In a large bowl, combine the leftover tagliatelle with cherry tomatoes, diced cucumber, thinly sliced red onion, torn fresh basil leaves, and halved Kalamata olives.
2. Drizzle olive oil and balsamic vinegar over the salad. Toss to combine.
3. Season with salt and black pepper to taste.
4. Let the flavors meld for about 10-15 minutes before serving, allowing the tagliatelle to absorb some of the dressing.
5. Serve the tagliatelle panzanella salad as a refreshing side dish or a light lunch.

These creative tagliatelle recipes are a testament to the versatility of leftovers. Whether you're enjoying a hearty tagliatelle frittata, indulging in tagliatelle-stuffed bell peppers, or savoring the freshness of a tagliatelle panzanella salad, these dishes show that repurposing leftover tagliatelle can lead to exciting and delicious new culinary experiences.

Chapter 19: Sweet Endings with Tagliatelle

Indulge your sweet tooth with these delectable dessert creations that reimagine tagliatelle in the realm of sweets. From a luscious Dessert Tagliatelle with Berries and Mascarpone, to whimsical Chocolate Hazelnut Tagliatelle Nests, and irresistible Cinnamon Sugar Tagliatelle Crisps, these recipes are the perfect way to conclude a meal on a delightful note.

Dessert Tagliatelle with Berries and Mascarpone

Dessert Tagliatelle with Berries and Mascarpone combines the elegance of tagliatelle with the vibrant flavors of fresh berries and the luxurious creaminess of mascarpone cheese.

Ingredients:

- Fresh tagliatelle pasta
- Fresh mixed berries (such as strawberries, blueberries, raspberries)
- Mascarpone cheese
- Honey or maple syrup
- Fresh mint leaves (for garnish)

Instructions:

1. Cook the tagliatelle in boiling water until al dente. Drain and set aside.
2. In a bowl, gently toss the cooked tagliatelle with fresh mixed berries.
3. Drizzle with honey or maple syrup and toss again to coat.

4. Serve the dessert tagliatelle in individual bowls, topped with dollops of mascarpone cheese.
5. Garnish with fresh mint leaves and extra berries, if desired.

Chocolate Hazelnut Tagliatelle Nests

Chocolate Hazelnut Tagliatelle Nests offer a playful and delightful dessert that combines the rich flavors of chocolate and hazelnuts with the visual appeal of nest-like creations.

Ingredients:

- Fresh tagliatelle pasta
- Nutella or chocolate hazelnut spread
- Hazelnuts, toasted and chopped
- Shredded coconut (optional)
- Edible flowers (for garnish, optional)

Instructions:

1. Cook the tagliatelle in boiling water until al dente. Drain and set aside.
2. Toss the cooked tagliatelle with Nutella or chocolate hazelnut spread until well coated.
3. Divide the coated tagliatelle into portions and shape each portion into a nest-like structure on serving plates.
4. Sprinkle toasted chopped hazelnuts and shredded coconut (if using) over the tagliatelle nests.
5. Garnish with edible flowers for an elegant touch.
6. Serve the chocolate hazelnut tagliatelle nests as a whimsical and delicious dessert.

Cinnamon Sugar Tagliatelle Crisps

Cinnamon Sugar Tagliatelle Crisps transform tagliatelle into a delightful crispy treat that's perfect for snacking or as a crunchy topping for other desserts.

Ingredients:

- Fresh tagliatelle pasta
- Butter, melted
- Cinnamon and sugar mixture
- Powdered sugar (for dusting)

Instructions:

1. Cook the tagliatelle in boiling water until al dente. Drain and set aside.
2. Toss the cooked tagliatelle with melted butter until well coated.
3. Spread the buttered tagliatelle in a single layer on a baking sheet.
4. Sprinkle the tagliatelle with the cinnamon and sugar mixture, ensuring even coverage.
5. Bake in a preheated oven at 350°F (175°C) for about 10-12 minutes, or until the tagliatelle crisps up and turns golden.
6. Remove from the oven and let the crisps cool.
7. Dust the cinnamon sugar tagliatelle crisps with powdered sugar before serving.

1. Enjoy as a sweet and crunchy treat.

These sweet endings with tagliatelle demonstrate the versatility of this pasta in the realm of desserts. Whether you're relishing the harmony of berries and mascarpone, enjoying the playful charm of chocolate hazelnut nests, or savoring the crispy delight of cinnamon sugar tagliatelle crisps, these recipes offer a delightful way to conclude your culinary journey with tagliatelle.

As we reach the end of this culinary journey through the world of tagliatelle pasta, we hope you've been inspired, delighted, and amazed by the countless possibilities that this versatile pasta offers. From classic Italian preparations to innovative twists, from savory to sweet, tagliatelle has proven itself to be a canvas for creativity and a vessel for flavor.

In this cookbook, we've explored the rich history and origin of tagliatelle, delved into essential tools and ingredients, mastered the art of tagliatelle dough, and ventured into a wide array of mouthwatering recipes spanning various cuisines, occasions, and dietary preferences. From the comfort of your kitchen, you've embarked on a culinary adventure that has taken you from the traditional to the extraordinary.

With each chapter, you've discovered the joy of crafting handmade tagliatelle, elevating your cooking skills, and delighting in the experience of preparing and savoring dishes that captivate the senses. The tagliatelle pasta cookbook has been your guide to exploring flavors, techniques, and inspirations that have transformed humble ingredients into exceptional meals.

We encourage you to continue experimenting, innovating, and sharing your love for tagliatelle with friends, family, and loved ones. May your kitchen continue to be a place of culinary exploration, creativity, and enjoyment.

Thank you for joining us on this delicious journey, and we look forward to seeing the incredible dishes you'll create with tagliatelle in the future. Buon appetito!